DIVERSITY, EQUITY, AND INCLUSION

DIVERSITY, EQUITY, AND INCLUSION

A Practical Guide

Anthony G. James, Jr.

Miami University

cognella®

SAN DIEGO

Bassim Hamadeh, CEO and Publisher
Amy Smith, Senior Project Editor
Abbey Hastings, Production Editor
Emely Villavicencio, Senior Graphic Designer
Stephanie Kohl, Licensing Coordinator
Natalie Piccotti, Director of Marketing
Kassie Graves, Senior Vice President of Editorial
Jamie Giganti, Director of Academic Publishing

Cover images: Copyright © 2020 iStockphoto LP/Prostock-Studio.
Copyright © 2020 iStockphoto LP/Prostock-Studio.

Printed in the United States of America.

cognella® | ACADEMIC PUBLISHING
3970 Sorrento Valley Blvd., Ste. 500, San Diego, CA 92121

Brief Contents

Detailed Contents

Foreword

Katherine S. Cho, Ph.D. (she/her)

B efore you is a primer for practicality. Efforts toward diversity, equity, and inclusion (DEI) often reveal interconnected, tangled, complex webs of systems and structures, differing perspectives, longstanding frustrations, and skepticism for actual, tangible change. As a result, trying to tackle or improve an organization's DEI efforts can be overwhelming.

What Dr. Anthony G. James, Jr., provides with his six-step model are questions, considerations, and examples to move us, as he writes, "from here to there." In doing this work through various roles and responsibilities, James and this primer emphasize the critical importance of how DEI are not destinations—these efforts must be tied to process and process tied to feedback so that their resultant outcomes are viewed as another step of *ongoing* change. To be clear, as outlined in chapters 3 and 4 of this book, you *should* have outcomes. However, as described, "the assumption here is that everyone knows 'what is right' or, more importantly, agrees with what that should be." In my own work studying organizational function (and arguably dysfunction) in addressing the concerns of students, staff, administrators, and faculty at colleges and universities, I see this quite often. Ask anyone in your organization, on your campus, at your office, about what should be done to improve the university (especially regarding DEI work), and you will likely have many different answers reflecting the diversity of our communities, our backgrounds, and our experiences of *belonging* (or, more often, the stories of how we were made to feel as though we *do not belong*). As a result, progress, depending on who you ask, will look like a hundred different things— and might look especially different between the people enacting the DEI work and the broader audience of individuals who are bearing the brunt of when DEI does not work. For this reason, I am especially appreciative of James's suggestion to integrate feedback and gaining perspective, perceptions, and input to *loop back* into the inevitable differences between the intent and the impact. For example, what is viewed as partnership and progress by some might be considered temporal appeasement or co-optation by others (see Cho, 2018).

The tension of recognizing DEI efforts as *both* process and outcomes, with the incorporation of feedback, ultimately gets to how we measure progress: How do we know we are moving forward? And again, with this question, James offers a critical consideration with time and the time horizon: We need not only clear benchmarks, but also the recognition and transparency regarding the complexity of addressing deeply rooted, often historicized pain with the importance of collaboratively setting and communicating realistic goals for organizational change. The way James considers progress as both journey and destination creates more space (i.e., options, abilities) for us to do, do *well*, and *keep* doing. Undergirding all of these chapters, in these efforts of doing, is how DEI efforts are a collective responsibility. Within his thoughtful recommendations and advice such as naming goals, understanding history, identifying account-ability mechanisms, and recognizing and celebrating communities, is the implicit recognition that all of the *doing* of DEI work cannot be on an individual level. Systemic, institutional issues require relational, collective, investment and an ethos of care grounded in building, building with one another and building in community. This book offers ways to build more thoughtfully, build more deeply, and build toward better realities.

Reference

Cho, K. S. (2018). The perception of progress: Conceptualizing institutional response to student protests and activism. *NEA Higher Education Journal: Thought and Action, 34*(1), 81–95.

Foreword

Darryl B. Rice, Ph.D.

Whether someone is seasoned diversity, equity, and inclusion (DEI) expert or a novice in the DEI space, there is something in the book for you. As a DEI scholar and educator, I am well aware of the challenges this work entails. The aspects that I enjoyed the most were (1) understanding what resources are needed to advance DEI and (2) knowing who is accountable for doing DEI. In organizational settings, these two aspects are often overlooked or minimized, which can frustrate and undermine efforts to advance DEI. It is one of the best DEI practical guides available and a resource I would gladly recommend.

Introduction

As a professor of higher education I frequently hear about diversity, equity, and inclusion (DEI) as a central component of the university mission. This makes sense, since many public universities attempt to equip students with human capital that allows them to make contributions to a culturally diverse world. Belief in the centrality of DEI extends even to the various professional organizations to which I have belonged (National Council on Family Relations, Society of Research on Child Development, and the Society for Research on Adolescence). That also makes sense, because these institutions provide a context for scholars to engage in research and practice that promotes the well-being of children, youth, and families.

Serving in these contexts has taught me that there are many facets to DEI, and that using some of the same processes I employ in my research may help support the goal of advancing a given area of DEI. The aim of this brief book is therefore to present a model for fostering DEI in a given context. Though most of the examples will derive from my experiences in higher education, the underlying model is flexible enough to be used in other fields such as corporate settings, nonprofit agencies, and social organizations—any group of individuals who desire to advance issues of diversity, equity, and inclusion. Its purpose is to help people clearly articulate their DEI-related goals and access a model for addressing them.

The model has six steps:

1. Identify the area of DEI to be addressed.
2. Articulate the intended outcomes.
3. Identify the metrics of change.
4. List and secure the resources needed to achieve expected outcomes.
5. Assign an entity or individual(s) to be accountable for the suggested change process.
6. Establish a clear time horizon.

Each step of the model occupies a chapter in this primer, with examples to bring the spirit of the model to life.

DEI-Related Experience

As with most leadership positions, it is important to note the experience of a given person in the realm or area for which they may be leading. In that spirit, I'll outline my DEI-related experiences and credentials.

At the time of this writing, I serve as the (interim) vice president for institutional diversity at Miami University. This role is akin to the more commonly used title of chief diversity officer of the institution. My responsibility includes being the central executive for strategy, collaboration, and planning for issues related to diversity, equity, and inclusion.

My first formal DEI role was in the military (U.S. Army National Guard). I served as the unit equal opportunity officer. Each unit had such an officer to address issues related to discrimination and harassment within the force. I completed this training in 2005 and served in that role for the remainder of my time while deployed to Iraq during the Operation Iraqi Freedom campaign. Primarily, my job was to investigate unfair treatment of soldiers and serve as an advisor to the company commander for such issues.

My next venture into this work was with the Missouri Department of Social Services, from approximately 2010–2012. The state of Missouri received an Annie E. Casey grant to examine issues of disproportionality and disparity across multiple phases of the child welfare systems (e.g., the rates at which youth of color entered the system, the level of care they received while their family was in the system, and the length at which they stayed in the system). The goal of the system was to protect children but also to try and reunify families. Because youth of color, particularly Black youth and their families, were entering the system at disproportionate rates and staying longer relative to other groups, the department moved forward with examining the extent to which race and racism accounted for the disparities. I served as a lead trainer for county agencies on issues of race and racism. And that was a 2-year project where the trainer talked about issues of race and racism with a goal of helping personnel examine practices and policies that create barriers to equity. This was very difficult work, particularly the fact that as an African American male I consistently found myself in areas where I was the only one who looked like me. However, I was able to have many meaningful conversations, especially after I was able to establish that we shared goals of ultimately providing care to children and families. And we were trying to remove barriers to those disproportionately impacted families across different ethnic groups.

Also, as a graduate student at the University of Missouri, I served as an executive of the Association of Black Graduate and Professional Students. In these roles I engaged graduated students in activities and conversations to help promote DEI across the campus. This was in concert with other student organizations and university faculty, staff, and administration. From there, I served on the Inclusion and Diversity Committee in my professional organization (National Council on Family Relations). This committee served as an advisory group to the board of directors, strategically examining strengths and weaknesses of diversity and inclusion across the organization. Equity in leadership, experience, and opportunities were at the heart of the work completed by this committee and provided me with valuable knowledge about the opportunities and constraints of promoting DEI in membership-based organizations.

At Miami University, I have served on the College of Education, Health, and Society, on the Diversity Advisory Group to the dean, and served as co-chair of the 2020 Presidential Task Force. The former served as an advisory group for the dean to consider college-level programming and initiatives related to DEI advancement, whereas the latter was a university-wide initiative examining the same.

What these experiences provided me was a diverse set of knowledge and competence about the opportunities and constraints facing advancing diversity, equity, and inclusion across several institutions and levels within each. Additionally, my military background provides me with general principles of leadership, as well as an ability to analyze problems and create plans and strategies to address the issues. Further, I am a faculty member who is a trained researcher of human development and family science. For the latter, developmental relational system approaches help guide my research and practice, including my DEI work. In sum, these factors shape my approach to tackling issues of diversity, equity, and inclusion. The goal of this primer text is to provide a model or framework to help others take a similar approach within their own institutional contexts.

Contextualizing University Structure

My primary role at Miami University is a faculty member. A major part of that role is to conduct independent research in my academic field (human development and family science). A major component to conducting research is contextualizing the problem under study. This is how complex phenomena are able to be described, examined, explained, and so on (Jaccard & Jacoby, 2019). In a practical sense, advancing DEI includes examination of the current state of diversity, equity, and inclusion in context, then coming up with the steps needed to make desired adjustments. This includes clearly articulating the current state of a given aspect of DEI (here) and clearly articulating the desired state of DEI in the same area (there). This is universal across institutions, though opportunities and constraints may certainly vary. Importantly, understanding the critical elements in the institution is a key first step. Because I am currently in a university setting, that will be used as the case example for the model being put forward in this text.

Universities typically have five or six key elements that create the structure of the institution: students, faculty, staff, administration, board of trustees and alumni. Within each, there are variations.

Students

For most institutions, students consist of the largest internal constituency of the institution. There are many different levels of students though. You have undergraduate students, graduate students, international students, low-income (e.g., Pell Grant eligible), part-time, full-time, commuter, residential, older adult, high school (e.g., some universities have articulation agreements with local high schools that allow those students to take college classes while in high school), and so on. This nonexhaustive list does not even get into issues of religion, race, ethnicity, sex, gender, and so on. The key is that each group, or the intersections of more than one, will create varying interest areas of a given group. So be cautious of language or narratives that group students into one collective. As this shows, there is much diversity in this group.

Faculty

Faculty is another constituency within institutions of higher learning. Again, there is also much diversity here. Faculty can consist of tenure-track (TT) and nontenure track (NTT) instructors, visiting assistant professors, adjuncts, graduate instructors, clinical lecturers, and so on. Each institution is likely to have varying names and labels to segment a given faculty member's role as it relates to the policy manual or state laws of the institution. What is important to one group within these categories may align with that of another category or may be qualitatively different. For instance, at research-intensive institutions, TT faculty may be concerned about their course loads (i.e., how many courses they are required to teach in a given term) and the extent to which it impacts their ability to engage in and publish high-impact research and/or qualify for merit pay raises. At the same institution, NTT faculty, who may not have as much of a focus on research (relative to TT faculty) but course/teaching load settings, how teaching loads are assigned, capacities for class sizes, how not focusing on research may impact their ability to qualify for merit pay raises, and so on are critical issues of great concern to this segment of the faculty. Part-time, or adjunct faculty, may be concerned about the pay differentials between their compensation for teaching a course (i.e., a set amount at most institutions) relative to what permanent faculty receive for teaching courses beyond their required course loads (i.e., typically some percentage of their base salaries). The difference between these two compensation structures can be thousands of dollars. The key is that these differences, or diversity, have the potential to create issues of equity and inclusion.

Staff

While faculty and students are likely what comes to mind when thinking about the individuals an institution of higher learning is composed of, much of the daily work of campus life is conducted by staff. This can include auxiliary services such as dining services, maintenance of physical facilities, financial services, residence advisors in residential halls, and so on. While there are likely all sorts of configurations and categories when dispersed across the many institutions of higher learning that exist, at Miami University these positions are dichotomized into classified (hourly wage) and unclassified (salaried) staff. They can also be distinguished based on their status as full-time or part-time employees. It is likely that many of these individuals work year-round at the campus and perform many of the daily operational functions of the university. Because they are on campus, they too contribute to the diversity of the institutional community and represent many identity categories. They also must feel included in the community and have access to reaching their full potential in their various areas of the institution.

Administrators

Administrators consist of the many personnel in the institution who have supervisory responsibility over others. This can be vice presidents, deans, provosts, staff supervisors such as director of student life, department chairs, and so on. In each case, issues of DEI are in some way or another part of the operations of work within these supervisory categories. It is for this reason that the federal government has the U.S. Equal Employment

Opportunity Commission to serve as an oversight group to ensure personnel are being treated fairly and have equal access to opportunities in the workplace. The many layers of personnel with supervisor personnel related decision-making authority is a major reason for having a clearly defined mechanism for addressing issues of DEI. This example is applicable to many or most institutions of higher learning but may not be for other institutions. The key for the diversity officer would be to identify the administrative structure within their institution and have a clear pathway to that individual's office.

Alumni

Alumni are another element of institution of higher learning. These are the ambassadors of the institution, as they have spent some amount of time at the institution and have completed (or maybe not completed) a program there. They, too, are segmented in all sorts of ways. For instance, there are alumni groups for a given major or college or academic group (e.g., Miami University Department of Comparative Religion), or alumni groups based on some other characteristic (e.g., Miami University 1806 LGBTQ alumni), extracurricular participation (e.g., equestrian team), and so on. The list can theoretically go on and on. The key thing to remember is that this is a group of ambassadors who care deeply and likely have an affinity and compassion that can help advance DEI efforts. Additionally, they may also have resources and connections that can be leveraged to advance the lived experience of internal members of the university community.

Governing Boards

Just about every institution has a governing body that has the fiduciary responsibility to continually monitor and make decisions to protect and engage the health of the institution. They can have a variety of names, but they are essentially the governing body (Tschirhart & Bielefeld, 2012). In public institutions, such as Miami University, they also represent the public as many of the members of the board of trustees (i.e., the name of the governing body at Miami University) are appointed by the governor, who is elected by the people. The main leadership of the institution (e.g., the president) reports to the board of trustees. The decisions made by the governing board certainly can impact DEI issues. For instance, if the board approves certain admission requirements, those requirements may ease entrance for some groups but at the same time constrain access to others. It is for such reasons that the diversity officer must be part of the governing body's decision-making processes to advise them on the intended and unintended consequences of their decisions.

Building Partnerships as a Mechanism of Fostering DEI

With any institution there will be elements or categories within it that are connected in some way. Using a system view, the manner in which those elements connect will determine whether and how diversity goals are met, the barriers to access or success, and the extent to which all members of the institutional community have a sense of belongingness. As an example, I use a university setting to show the importance of partnerships and connection as a mechanism to fostering DEI goals.

Given there are so many stakeholders in an institution of higher learning—students, faculty, alumni, administrators, staff, governing boards, the local community—and that they sometimes have conflicting interests, DEI work can get complex very quickly. External events can influence the level of interest in DEI, too, even if no one in the organization has a direct connection to those events. They may remind people of what their own experiences have been like. Further, universities are embedded in political environments where events related to DEI goals can also impact the extent to which people feel the institution is sensitive to the needs of all members in the community, particularly those on the margins. A good example is the murders of George Floyd, Breonna Taylor, and Aumad Arbery.

Every stakeholder or group is not necessarily going to have the same perspective on events like these or agree with the approach that an institution take in response to the event. The key issue of concern for leaders in the institution, particularly chief diversity officers, is to be mindful of and sensitive toward those directly impacted by such political events. This is a critical part of the feeling of belongingness embedded in the inclusive portion of DEI. At the same time, there is a need for leaders to be sensitive to the varying perspectives on the events, even those in opposition to narratives and views by others in the same community. Privileging one group more than others increases tension and can derail DEI goals.

Achieving balance doesn't necessarily mean giving everyone equal time or picking a side. The key is to stay attuned to stakeholders' lived experiences and continually engage in removing barriers to communication and understanding, which ultimately influences the lived experience of all stakeholders in the community. The difficulty of this is that in one institution there can be many groups or individuals that have sharp differences in aspects of DEI they focus on; how the university should respond to instances of bias, bigotry, and hate; the extent to which their voice is heard, and so on.

A collaborative, from-the-ground-up approach will focus on empowering different stakeholders and building partnerships, because no single person or position of authority can satisfy everyone's needs and demands. To which components of your organization are you already connected, and with which do you need to forge a connection, and how? Do you have, or can you create, a structure in which people can better understand what their own responsibility for DEI is and where and how to get involved outside of that? How will you hold yourself and others accountable?

Building relationships across key stakeholders is one way to help people identify the structures of the institution as it relates to DEI goals but also where they can get involved and ensure their voice is heard. In a well-structured DEI system, this should be the case from the lowest levels of the institution up to its upper echelons of leadership. Moreover, this allows for smooth bidirectional exchanges of information, which can be continuously monitored by the entity responsible for DEI at the institution.

Conceptualizing DEI

Let's clearly define the elements of DEI before we go on to talk about the steps in the model.

Diversity

At its core, diversity simply means the existence of differences across characteristics, attributes, perspectives, and so on. Miami University, my current employer, views diversity holistically, understanding that the definition is constantly evolving. It includes but is not limited to race, ethnicity, color, nationality, sex, sexual orientation, gender identity and expression, class, religion, ability, age, military status, visa status, economic status, geographic location, and language/linguistic ability. Diverse and well-reasoned ideas, approaches, and experiences are also essential parts of inclusion and equity. And this doesn't begin to touch on the complexity implied by intersectionality, in which people differ on more than one of these characteristics.

Diversity also means there are special interest groups to be mindful of. Acknowledging their existence and their role in a given context is important even if we are not able to satisfy them completely. You are probably beginning to see where the complexity of DEI comes in.

Equity

Equity ensures that everyone has access to the same opportunities. It recognizes that advantages and barriers exist and that as a result we don't all start from the same place. It begins by acknowledging that unequal starting place and goes on to correct and address the imbalance.

Fostering equity is about removing barriers so that people are able to self-actualize or reach their full potential. For example, my university is a public institution that represents the state of Ohio. Those barriers can range from family economic circumstances, the quality of education provided in the district where the student attends schools, the costs of the institution, the admission requirements at the institution, and so on. The key for any institution is to examine the processes they have in place that may add barriers to the typical student gaining access to the institution. Some barriers are in the control of the institution (e.g., admissions requirements) and others are not (e.g., whether an institution aligns with the geographic desires of potential students such as the institution being in a rural area but the student wants a more urban experience).

In theory, any student in the state should be able to enroll, do well, and graduate, but there are barriers. You probably have a list of barriers that exist at your own institution. Just write them in your notes for now. But know that if you can identify and then remove them, you will be creating access and opportunities for each person who has the chance or desire to be in that space.

Inclusion

Inclusion is the confidence of having a place in the institution or feeling like one belongs. If you're the only one who looks or acts as you do, if nothing reflects who you are or your core sense of self, you don't feel a sense of inclusion, and that's uncomfortable and can impact your success in the institution (Gopalan & Brady, 2020; O'Reilly et al., 2015). You don't feel like you belong. How do we make sure that each person who steps on campus feels the embrace of inclusion, has a group or a place where they are seen as, and respected for, who they are? The larger your institution, the more challenging it is to ensure that place. As important and welcome as they are, diversity of thought, diversity of ideas, diversity of traditions, and so forth can also hinder our ability to allow people to fully be themselves within a given context. Let's focus on how this may work for students at an institution of higher education.

Students are anxious to belong, and their parents want them to belong. At a university, as anywhere, the hope is that you create the conditions in which all members can find their space, where their humanity will be respected and they will feel a sense of dignity. It doesn't take much to disrupt that: a negative image posted on social media brings the emails of sharp critique, and institutional leaders have to figure out what to do about it. Why? Because this impacts the sense of belongingness of students (and faculty/staff) and the extent to which they are successful in the institution. The is the systemic nature of doing DEI work in diverse organizations. We'll talk more about this process later in the text.

The Dynamic Nature of Doing DEI

Finally, let us move on to discuss an important aspect of doing, or engaging, DEI work. A key phenomenon to keep in mind is that of understanding process versus outcome (Rossi et al., 2018). This is a concept that has heavy usage in program evaluation, but when considering that a significant part of DEI work includes monitoring empirical trends and implementing programming to promote equity and inclusion, it is important to understand distinctions between process and outcome elements.

Process Versus Outcome

Both process and outcome are important concepts in the world of evaluation research (Tschirhart & Bielefeld, 2012). In short, process regards the extent to which program activities are designed and implemented as intended and results in certain outputs. Outcome refers to whether the program affected aspects of the population that it intended to address. For example, let's say that an institution of higher learning wanted to increase their enrollment of students representing a given ethnic or racial background. The actual enrollment statistics would be the outcome in this example. The process would be the activities implemented in impacting change in those numbers.

Assumptions

Assumptions guide all human action (Ford & Lerner, 1992), and this includes human efforts toward advancing DEI. My goal here is not to articulate all the possible assumptions that undergird DEI efforts, but rather to strongly encourage you to clearly identify and reflect on the assumptions underlying your desire for given DEI outcomes. Assumptions, like values and other factors, will clearly influence the structure of those desired outcomes and the processes you choose to achieve them. In short, if the assumptions are incorrect, much like not meeting the assumptions of a regression analysis (Osborne & Waters, 2002), the efforts to advance DEI will fail.

Always check your assumptions. I don't mean check as in putting them aside. I mean check them in terms of understanding the assumptions on which you are basing your decisions. Here's an example: One piece of language I typically hear when incidents of harm occur on campus is that the university should "do what is [morally] right." It is in this spirit that suggestions for DEI-related change are born. However, in a complex organization (such as an institution of higher learning) what is considered morally right is not as clear-cut as someone may assume. This creates tensions across varying members of the community, even decision-making units, about what changes should be considered, or even if they should. Understanding the diversity of beliefs, values, and thoughts of what is morally right in your institution, will help prepare leaders for the type of pushback or support they receive when they start down such a path of addressing how the university responds to incidents of harm. The assumption here is that everyone knows "what is right" or, more importantly, agrees with what that should be. If I may offer some advice: The more diverse your institution, the more likely it is that there will be wide variation in what is considered "what is right."

The takeaway point here is that assumptions about some given DEI-related issue are likely guiding your action in that area. That's fine. But it's also important to see that other people in your institution may be operating under different assumptions, or even vastly different visions about how the world ought to work (Sowell, 2002). And those differences can create some tensions.

Disproportionality and Disparity

People use the words *disproportionality* and *disparity* as a guide for desiring change. However, people may not understand what these terms mean or the extent to which processes can be adjusted to actually change outcomes on some given DEI category.

Disproportionality

Disproportionality means there is a varying between some category in a given context relative to the actual numerical representation of that category in the larger population. That's a mouthful. Let me give an example. In the state of Ohio, depending on which metric you use (e.g., Black or African American or combination of the two such as Black/African American), the African American population is either 12 or 14% of the total state population. However, Black/African American students represent approximately 4% of the student population at Miami University, a public institution of higher education in the state of Ohio. Thus, this represents a disproportionality between the representation of that group in the state, relative to their representation in population at Miami University. This, for some, may elicit desires for changes (i.e., increasing the percentage of that group of students at Miami University to be more representative of their proportion of representation in the state where the institution is housed).

Disparity

Disparity regards comparative rates of success/failure on some given outcome. For example, let's use graduation rates at Miami University. Miami University has students representing a variety of racial/ethnic backgrounds. There are variations across these groups in the duration in which those groups (as a whole) spend at the university and ultimately graduate with their given degree. These variations create the rates of difference (or disparity) when compared. At Miami University (2018), the 2018–2019 fact sheet shows that the 6-year graduation rate for the 2012 cohort had and overall rate of 80% (meaning 80% of the students from that cohort graduated from the institution by the end of the 2017–2018 academic year. However, a disaggregation of the data also shows differential 6-year graduation rates across racial/ethnic groups (i.e., 27% Black/African American, 68% Hispanic/Latino, 81% White, 82% Asian, etc.). These data are interpreted as a racial and/or ethnic disparity in the 6-year graduation rate among Miami University students, which can elicit desires to enact changes to produce more equalized results across the groups. To be fair, there are other ways of calculating disparities. For instance, you can look at a number of people in a given category representing some category per 100,000 in the population.

The key with either disparities or disproportionality is to what extent discrimination accounts for, or is the cause of, the given disparity. Though it certainly comes with its controversies, Thomas Sowell (2019) explores how common disparities are across contexts and the extent to which scarce resources should be employed to close them. To the extent that social process are responsible for creating barriers that feed into disparities, there is a strong argument to make adjustment to the processes to provide equal opportunities for all members in a given context or institution. It is at that time that such a framework, as outlined before, can help address the important questions of whether and/or how a given intended outcomes can be addressed or should be.

Paradox of Diversity

It is also important for me to mention something about the work of DEI that sometimes get veiled in discussions of diversity, which his that there is also a paradox of diversity. The paradox is that the more diverse the context, the more opportunity there are for misunderstandings and between-group tensions because each of those diverse groups have histories and whims, preferences, and values that can be qualitatively different from the other group's (Sowell, 2019). When these groups are forced to live together in some given bounded context, those differences can be difficult to manage. Why? Because they are fighting for a variety of scarce resources (e.g., space, money, policy decision) that best align with or represent their values, which may be vastly different from what other group desires or values. So, the more diverse the community, the more difficult it can be to manage those differences and the tensions that result from those differences. This is why calls for more diversity may not produce less tensions but may actually strengthen them. It's a paradox. For instance, people in a given institution may call for more diversity and at the same time they also put forward stiff critiques about the diversity-related problems that currently exist in the community, which are a result of diversity. This is an issue that deserves more attention, or at least consideration in decisions about diversity.

To be sure, I'm not saying let's not have more diversity, because it's going to bring problems. What I'm saying is that understanding that more diversity creates more opportunities for tension across differences in attributes, for example, potentially results in more tensions in a given setting. There has to be a mechanism in place to effectively to manage that and manage it well. The only way to avoid this is to have a sort of fairy tale situation where all of those groups in your context share the same values, histories, and preferences, which is unlikely to be the case. In my institution, we have students who may come from rural, Appalachian Ohio, and we also have students who may come from urban hipster contexts. They each have different ways of living, different values, different ideas about how policy should work, and so on. Those differences have to be managed because they can produce cultural clashes that make one group feel less valued or ignored or alienated or offended at certain actions by members of other groups. Being mindful of such potential strife and having a plan in place to address is it is one value add of having a diversity officer who thinks critically about such issues.

Concluding Thoughts

The model I'll outline in the following chapters doesn't promise you'll achieve the DEI results you seek. Instead, it's a mechanism you can put in a place to see *whether your intended changes are occurring.* For many people who have worked a long time in this field, myself included, the feeling that nothing has changed over time is quite frustrating. But when people tell me nothing has changed, my first question is usually, "What processes have you put in place to *measure* the change?" or "What time period are you evaluating to determine if any change has occurred?" This is usually where I get a lot of puzzled looks in response.

My hope is that having a model in which you can plug in your goals and measure the outcomes will help you see when things have, in fact, changed. The model does not promise outcomes, but it at least allows you to clarify the plan. It also makes it easy to see what's realistically possible. As hard as it is to step up and say, "I'm not sure that's something we can achieve," in some situations change is simply out of our control. On the other hand, suppose the number of incoming students in particular groups has looked flat for decades and there are aspects of recruitment and admissions processes that can be adjusted to increase those numbers. At the very least, having a process to examine this feasibility puts the institution on the right path to potentially remove barriers contributing to the flat numbers. Also keep in mind that statistics can be tricky (Wheelan, 2013).

For instance, if you combine some groups, the numbers may show that representation of a given group *has* grown a little (e.g., using African American or Black as opposed to African American and Black as a combined group). So, it depends on which metric you're using, which group of students you're interested in increasing. But it's not until you identify your goals that you can start putting some plans and metrics into place that will let you track the extent to which you're actually reaching those goals.

Another essential goal for leaders doing work in this realm is being transparent about DEI efforts and helping all members of a given community better understand the decision to pursue a given outcome. Many people have DEI-related ideas and suggestions that are great in theory but impossible to put into practice. Developing the mechanisms and structure that usher in opportunities to facilitate change requires clearly articulating the steps you've planned to reach the desired outcome. The model presented in this text helps to that end.

If your ideas for DEI-related change cannot be mapped into the six-stage model, it may be best not to put them forward as a recommendation to DEI leaders, because they are likely to have a high failure rate or at least not deliver the intended outcomes. The model's processes not only point our eyes and hopes toward desired change; they also prevent us from being blinded by unintended effects, a flaw that has historically derailed the advancement of DEI efforts (Mac Donald, 2018). Finally, it is essential to note that all DEI-related goals, like other human action (Ford & Lerner, 1992), are undergirded by assumptions, and it is important to understand them and how they potentially impact DEI-related intended changes.

Now let's look at the first step, identifying the DEI goal.

1

What Is the Diversity Characteristic You Want to Change?

A cross many corporations and institutions, diversity, equity, and inclusion (DEI) have been important aspects of the mission. However, enacting changes that produced the desired outcomes has generally been a process that left much to be desired. My hope is that this primer will assist such entities with a model for enacting changes that produce desired outcomes. Or, at the very least, it puts forward a mechanism for understanding the opportunities and constraints to reaching given DEI-related outcomes.

However, this requires clearly identifying the area of diversity in which the change is desired. Identifying a goal like this is complicated by the fact that human contexts can be diverse in all sorts of ways. Typically, people think of racial, ethnic, religious, disability, gender, and sexuality as the main characteristics of diversity. However, one technological firm lists nearly 34 diversity characteristics on its website (Reiners, 2020). Thus, it is critically important for individuals to identity the specific characteristic of diversity they seek to change in a given context. Not least among the reasons for being so specific is that it can be notoriously difficult to make changes across all the categories of diversity all at once.

In addition to identifying the specific diversity characteristic, say disability, we must clearly conceptualize (or be precise) about what that means in our context. First, which type of disability? Reiners (2020) lists two: cognitive and physical. These two types not only have different structural impacts on individuals; they are also open to different responses, such as adding ramps in front of buildings versus making sure PDF files are accessible to those who cannot readily identify certain colors or patterns. This short example highlights the need to clearly and precisely articulate the component of disability in question and also conceptualize what that means in a given context.

The vast variation in diversity has many components (race, ethnicity, sexualities, religion, disability, gender, and so on), and the extent of each of these will vary across groups. One of the more difficult tasks of doing DEI work is identifying priorities. Thus, the first step of my model is clearly identifying and articulating the current state of diversity or the component of DEI in a given bounded context (higher education, corporate business). In the second step, I identify the current state of DEI in the bounded context with respect to that element of DEI. In other words, as a leader doing the DEI work, you should always be thinking about where you are and where you are trying to go. The latter will be the focus of the second chapter. A quick example takes us back to the enrollment rates of Black and/or Black/African American students at Miami University. On one hand, you can combine the groups or you can disaggregate them (U.S. Department of Labor, n.d.). Then you have to determine what the enrollment rates are, and possibly have historically been, in the institution. From that, leaders or community members can determine if those rates are sufficient and whether or how to address them. Sometimes you also have to consider things such if you are looking at this at a given campus in the institution, across campuses, in given division, and so on. Again, precision is the key.

Different organizations or units or divisions can have different goals about diversity. Being able to clarify what those are is helpful because then you can position resources in a way that helps you achieve your end point or desired outcomes. These latter points will be discussed in subsequent chapters.

Keep in mind that complex and highly diverse contexts have many reasons for why they operate the way they do. Suggesting changes to that system will likely have some feedback loops that are not always aligned with the desired changes. This is a key aspect of systems theory (e.g., James, 2020). Thus, it is prudent for leaders to clearly articulate the undergirding rationale for why they desire changes in a given area of DEI, hopefully linking such changes to the strategic mission and visions of the institution (Tschirhart & Bielefeld, 2012).

QUESTIONS TO CONSIDER

1. What aspect of diversity are you seeking to change in the institution?

2. For the given area of DEI you seek to change at the institution, what is the current state of affairs? What are the historical trends?

3. What rationale are you using as a basis for the desired DEI-related changed?

4. What assumptions are you making about the need to advance DEI-related change in the institution?

2

What Are Your Intended Outcomes?

Articulate the intended changes (outcomes) for this area of the institution and the rationale for them. For instance, maybe the status quo, or current state of a given DEI area, is misaligned with the mission of the university. Again, this requires institutional leaders to spell out where the institution is (the "here") and where we want the institution to be in the future (the "there"). This specifies the intended direction. Additionally, it would strengthen the argument being made if leaders were able to identify and present any evidence to support advancing DEI in a given context.

Let's say you identified the here (current state of affairs). Now where do you want to go (desired future state of affairs)? Let's stick with the same example we've previously used, enrollment of Black/African American students at the institution. Suppose you want to enroll more students representing this racial/ethnic category. Leaders at your institution made the decision that the current state of affairs is insufficient or does not align with the mission of the institution. Several ideas related to this step in the model are worth considering.

Support or Rationale for Desired Outcome

This now brings up the question of what serves as the guiding force for answering what a sufficient rate should be. Of course, we could use proportionality in terms of what proportion of the state population that racial/ethnic group represents. Either way, it would be helpful to clearly and precisely identify that targeted outcome. Please note that everyone may not necessarily agree with the targeted outcome, and there is likely to be some stiff criticism awaiting if the targeted outcome is not reached. This is multiplied if there is not a sound reason for pursuing a given outcome.

Unintended Consequences

Not having good reason for changes can produce undesirable outcomes, or unintended consequences. To be sure, intentionally trying to reach a given DEI outcome has proven to be a difficult venture. One author argues that such ventures are delusional (Mac Donald, 2018). However, more balanced approaches honestly study the feasibility of diversity-related goals. Dobbin and Kalev (2016) list many areas of promise (task forces, diversity managers, self-management) and concern (mandatory training, grievance systems, testing) as they relate to reaching future DEI-related outcomes. What this study means is that leaders must think prudently about the unintended consequences (or outcomes) that may arise in the pursuit toward the desired outcomes.

The key takeaway is that leaders need to clearly and precisely identify a direction for their DEI-related goals and a good reason for taking such an approach. As the infamous quotation says, if you don't know where you're going, you'll probably end up somewhere else (Campbell, 1990). That's what happens if you don't have direction. This is true, even in the DEI realm.

QUESTIONS TO CONSIDER

1. Why do you, or your institution, desire the DEI related change being sought after?
2. What aspect of DEI are you not satisfied with?
3. What rationale, or support, are you basing your dissatisfaction with the current state of affairs?
4. What evidence, facts, or support do you have to believe that engaging in some given process in a desired DEI-related area leads to the outcome you desire?
5. What would the state of affairs in a given DEI-related area need to be in order for you or your institution to be satisfied?

3

What Are the Metrics of Change?

We've identified what we want to change. We know where we are and where we want to go. The next step in the model is to identify the metrics we'll use to periodically measure the extent of the intended changes. To be sure, it is completely feasible to use the same metric, discussed earlier, that was used to identify the current state of affairs in the given DEI area. There are a few things to consider.

Authentication Processes Are Important

One factor that explains that the failure of social policy is the result of its being protected from authentication processes (Sowell, 2008). Authentication creates an accountability mechanism for decision makers that motivates them to make decisions that maximize their opportunity of success. To that end, the model presented here argues that all proposals for advancing DEI should have an authentication process that holds the decision makers accountable.

Don't Just Chase Quotas

Likely one of the first questions leaders should ask is what we should use as a metric to measure change in the given area of DEI. Beware of chasing quotas! This is illegal and will get you in the news for the wrong reason. And you don't want to measure just positive change, but even negative change and unintended consequences.

Incremental Approaches

It is sufficient to also use an incremental approach on the pathway of reaching a desired outcome. This work is not easy, and it can be costly, so it is prudent to pilot an idea and then move forward if the measurable change is in the right direction. This approach also takes account of a systems view (James, 2020), which asserts that change in one part of a system has reverberating effects in other parts of the system. Taking a prudent and systemic incremental approach allows leaders to cease advancing DEI if changes signal unintended consequences. Not realizing this early enough, or after wholesale (or categorical; Sowell, 2008) changes can be quite detrimental. What this approach provides is a feedback mechanism or feedback loop to signal whether change is moving in the right direction. Let me provide an example.

Suppose an institution of higher learning enrolls a group of students from a particular racial or ethnic background and scarce resources or programming reflect their cultural heritage. Those students have a negative experience and drop out or finish and harbor significant negative feelings toward the institution. Those individuals are likely to take that information back to their community and say, "Look, I don't care where you go. Just don't go there." That doesn't help the institution, especially if a desired DEI-related goal is to increase the enrollment of students matching those who previously had negative experiences.

It is for this reason that institutions need to have a comprehensive plan that encourages thinking about the system as a whole. For an institution of higher learning, this means that for students, from recruiting to onboarding, helping them transition into a career and be positive ambassadors of the institution is part of the full experience of completing a program at the organization. Such feedback loops can answer questions such as "How well is the plan working? What was the experience positive or negative for those impacted by it in the institution? What did focus group or survey data reveal about the changes enacted?" and so on. These are feedback loops that help leaders evaluate the extent to which the DEI-related changes are moving in the right direction.

Putting accountability measures in place may increase the odds of success. If no one holds the leaders of the DEI-related changes accountable, or examines the metrics, there may be more room for being a little more lax about implementing changes that advance efforts toward the desired outcomes.

QUESTIONS TO CONSIDER

1. What metrics will you use to evaluate DEI-related change over time?

2. Are you taking a categorical or incremental approach in the changes?

3. Have you identified milestones that signal desired changes in the process from start to completion?

4. What feedback loops have you identified to signal desired or undesired change?

4

What Resources Are Needed to Enact Changes?

A djusting the diversity of personnel, establishing equal opportunities in processing, and making sure all community members feel a sense of belonginess can be a costly venture. Thus, it is important to identify the expected resources, or costs, needed to enact those changes (European Commission, 2003). Of course, it is important to note that cost-benefit analysis can be helpful at determining what the costs would be to enact some given DEI-related change and whether it is worth pursuing. This, of course should happen before the process starts. If a decision is made to start without a clear understanding of the costs, the harm done may be more significant than having never made the decision in the first place (Sowell, 2008). Of course, there are some factors to consider in these processes.

Determining the Resources Needed to Advance DEI

This step in the model concerns fully determining and listing the resources needed to advance DEI in a given area. It is prudent to keep in mind that costs are not always financial. In my field we talk about resources in terms of time, energy, and human capital; knowledge; and so on. People with a particular background, a certain knowledge set, or relevant skills can also serve as a resource. Additionally, you have to have resources in place to support advancement of DEI or have a plan to get them into place. This may involve hiring personnel, which is costly (European Commission, 2003). Up to this point the assumption may be that all resources are in the control or realm of your institution. This is not necessarily the case.

Also think about scarcity. What makes something a valued resource is the fact that it's scarce, that you can't have all of it that you desire. For example, Miami University has a very good faculty, but because of our classification as a research institution we get plucked by the bigger institutions who can pay a little bit more and can guarantee faculty a research space. So for us, faculty can be a scarce resource. So now you have to think about how you position your scarce resources. That can mean planning some changes over the next few years that are painful to make, but the hope is to position or reposition our resources in a way that makes us stronger, that makes us more agile when the next crisis hits, which is bound to happen at some time.

I also have to think more comprehensively about the resources I do have available. Here, for instance, I think about how Miami University can combine our resources in a way that allows people to be the superstars they are in their fields but also be able to resist some of those calls from larger institutions when they come, because if you're good, people are going to find you. That's a challenge; it's an issue of scarcity, so it would be a mistake to only consider the resources you have but not consider that what you have is scarce. And you have to be able to use it in a way that's going to allow you to position yourself in the best way to meet your strategic priorities.

An important part of this discussion is that these changes may not happen overnight. However, it is important for leaders to be able to pro-vide spaces on campus (what is in their control) to meet the needs of the current diversity while also building toward meeting the needs of the diversity the community desires to see in the future, maybe by working with campus stores to get product that students from minority groups are not able to get from places out in the community.

Addressing Resource Costs Outside Your Institution

One example that comes to mind, which employs a systems perspective (James, 2020; Sowell, 2008), involves what is available to community members who choose your institution. Some years ago, a colleague of mine conducted exit interviews with African American students who didn't return to our campus the following year. When asked why they were transferring, these students said, "Oh, I have fun on campus. That was fine. It's just the local Walmart didn't have my hair products." That may seem trivial, but it was meaningful enough that it convinced students to seek other institutions that better met their personal needs. It may be that during the planning process for the influx of African American students no one thought of calling Walmart to maybe suggest stocking the shelves with products that meet the unique needs of incoming students. So why not call your local stores to simply ask if they could possibly stock or increase the types of products these students are going to need?

Another issue outside one's control is geographic location. One of the things I get asked the most by folks who don't live here in southwest Ohio is what it is like to live with palm trees around. And I have to tell them that we're in Ohio. We're not the University of Miami, which is in Florida. After we get through that, they may say, "How do you like living in Oxford?" These questions are meaningful too, say when hiring faculty and staff. I've served on several faculty search committees and people ask, "Do I have to live in Oxford?" And that's a challenge we have to talk through because we want to make sure it's a place where people are comfortable and want to be there. We want them to participate and come to events on campus, not just do their work and then leave. If that happens, they are also taking away from the campus some of those very resources we need (i.e., faculty of color who are engaged in the local campus and/or community). People showing up in a space can be a resource in terms of increasing the presence of diverse communities. These factors can easily be forgotten if you don't have a comprehensive plan, or if you don't have the right people at the table to understand what the needed resources are. But they matter because they help create a balance between the current state of affairs at your institution and what leaders desire it to be.

QUESTIONS TO CONSIDER

1. What resources are available to advance DEI?
2. What resources are needed to advance DEI in a given area?
3. What resources need to be addressed that are outside the institution?

5

Who Is Accountable for the DEI-Related Changes?

The next step in the model is to clearly identify the party or entity that will be responsible for the DEI-related goal or outcome. This should not be a random selection; rather, each DEI-related goal should be housed in a part of the institution that is most responsible for the processes related to making the change. That entity has the knowledge to best plan out the work to be done and help address aforementioned steps in the model. For instance, a center on campus focusing on student diversity and inclusion is likely the entity accountable for programming available to students that covers diverse topics and is inclusive. There are some things to consider.

Structure of Diversity and Inclusion

One consideration or identifying the accountable parties in the institution for given DEI-related goals is to better understand the structure of diversity and inclusion at your institution. Where are certain individuals, groups, and centers housed that regularly focus on these sorts of issues? This will also illumine the leaders of these areas and their position in the institution. The structure of DEI and their position in the institution can also signal the level of support that will be provided for pursuing DEI goals. If there is no buy-in from upper administration for the DEI-related goals, being able to carry them out with authority will be difficult. There is not one way of doing DEI work in an institution. How universities are structured vary widely. In fact, I challenge you to randomly select, say, seven to 10 colleges or universities in your state. Then, simply compare the structure (e.g., what programs they focus on, what staff positions they have, what areas of diversity are prioritized, if there is a diversity officer(s) in upper administration, etc.) across those institutions. Because I have done this myself, my hunch is that you too will also find that there is wide variation for how offices are structured. More opaque are communication processes across DEI-related entities in the institutions.

Also keep in mind that DEI-related work can be housed in one centralized office or spread out across multiple units in the institution. Again, the key point to remember is not that there is a universally approved way for structuring DEI, but rather that each institution has to determine if their current structure allows them to promote diversity, equity, and inclusion in a way that meets their DEI-related goals.

Be Collaborative

When discussing systems processes in complex institutions, such as universities and colleges, being able to develop and maintain collaborative partners across campus will be essential to the success of the diversity-related goals. Make sure that standing DEI-related committees have a mechanism to communicate with each other and work collaboratively toward a shared unit and university DEI goals. The success or failure of being able to pursue and reach DEI outcomes will in part be based on the extent to which you are able to partner with local resident experts for those given areas. Being able to have their support can help with buy-in and understanding the nuances, potential, and consequences of pursuing certain goals or pursuing them in given way. When people can see that you're sincere, that you're really trying to improve some aspect of DEI, as are they, that likely promotes some trust, freedom, flexibility, and opportunity to develop a plan and to try it out. In short, be collaborative.

Also be prepared to work with individuals in your same institution who have vastly different visions about DEI-related goals or even pathways to reaching those goals. For the former, those individuals may wholeheartedly disagree that a given goal is worth pursuing. Depending on their status, knowledge, expertise, and position in the institution, they can derail the process before it ever gets started. Similarly, a given person or entity may share the DEI-related outcome but disagree with the pathway to getting there. Again, depending on the aforementioned factors, this too can stall progress. For both, being able to work collaboratively, even with those who disagree on goals or pathways, can potentially lead to a compromise everyone can agree on, to help move the institution toward the DEI goal.

QUESTIONS TO CONSIDER

1. What person or entity will be responsible for the DEI-related goal? In lay terms, where does the buck stop?
2. Where will the responsibility of doing the DEI-related work be housed?
3. Who will be the point person for check-ins to monitor progress on the goals?
4. Who will be responsible for regularly monitoring the progress of the DEI-related goals?

6

What Is the Time Horizon?

The next step in the model concerns the time horizon for each of the desired DEI-related changes. More specifically, articulate a clear time horizon for the intended change so that you can evaluate movement toward the goal. Develop an evaluation schedule that includes benchmarks between the here and there.

A common complaint against DEI-related efforts is that they die or become irrelevant. One part of the reason for such complaints is that there is not a clear time horizon associated with how long the efforts are to last or when desired outcomes and results should be expected. Employing a mechanism to provide such information also creates some accountability, or at least motivation, to make progress within a given amount of time. Several other considerations are also important.

Determining the Time Horizon

There is no absolute answer to determining the time horizon that I am aware of; however, working with the entity(s) that will be held accountable for the given DEI-related change is one approach. It is likely that the entity responsible for the change will have some knowledge about how long it may take to actually reach the desired outcome. The goal is to try realizing the goal. Select some future check-in points (e.g., 6 months, 1 year, 18 months, etc.) and communicate progress and monitor feedback loops that indicate whether efforts should be altered, ceased, or continued. For instance, at my university I was able to place the diversity of faculty staff and students on our Institutional Diversity and Inclusion website.

That allowed for community members to see the historical trends (i.e., 10 years in this case) and monitor if they are moving in the right direction and whether actionable steps need to be taken to adjust the numbers in some way.

Another approach is to create backward plan approach, which has been used in several education-related areas. However, this was also a primary approach to mission planning that I used during my military career. Briefly, the idea is to start with the desired goal, outcome, or objective. Then plan backward from there using knowledge about various steps to determine the amount of time it would take the reach that point in the project. Once all of the steps are identified, from the objective back to the starting point (i.e., backward design or planning), adding up the time it takes to get from step to step reveals the approximate time it will take to realize the DEI-related goal. This becomes the time horizon for the goal.

Be Realistic and Reasonable

It is worth stating that DEI-related change can be difficult for a variety of reasons. Those reasons are likely responsible for possible reluctance by the party ultimately accountable for the DEI-related goal to buy into the plan to pursue it, which can possibly motivate them to not be forthcoming about realistic time horizon goals. For instance, it may be the case that the entity responsible for the party has some key piece of knowledge about the feasibility of making such changes, or the history about why things are the way they are. The current state of affairs may actually be progress toward a goal that is more advanced than previous points. However, without institutional memory of the DEI-related area in a given institution it is difficult to realize why the current state of affairs is where it is and the work it took to get to that point. In short, don't allow frustration with the current state of affairs to overshadow the fact that progress can be slow and incremental for many reasons not publicly known. A more reasonable and realistic approach is to work in concert with the accountable entity, work collaboratively to identify the benefit of pursuing the DEI goal, employ the steps for this model to show the collaborative approach being taken, and establish a realistic time horizon. Lastly, keep in mind that some changes do not go as planned, and undoing them can be difficult or even impossible. This is why it is important to consider a systemic, incremental approach to making DEI-related changes to avoid missteps that not only veer the DEI goals off path, but also result in unintended consequences that do more harm than if the changes were never attempted in the first place. Be realistic and reasonable in working with collaborative partners. I assume that most leaders would rather be prudent and right than haste and irreversibly wrong.

Focus on Process

A key part of diversity and inclusion work is the processes and policies in place to make sure that the community is diverse, provides equal opportunity, and engages in actions that make members of the institutional community feel a sense of belonging. This requires having processes that, to the greatest extent, assure these outcomes. Developing processes, monitoring processes, changing processing, and evaluating effectiveness all take time. The key question is how much time. Developing a process that allows you to determine a time horizon also has the added benefit of helping your agency be consistent in how it addresses issues in the institution or considers requests to pursue given DEI-related goals. For instance, suppose some policies are put in a place; they don't meet their intended outcomes, but then they harden into expectations. And when people feel entitled about anything it's hard to take it away from them. You have to be courageous enough to call things off, to say this isn't working and we need to go in a different direction. When process is the focus, this is easier to do and provides some grounding for leaders to be able to make the decision with confidence and sound reasoning.

QUESTIONS TO CONSIDER

1. Have you reached out to the accountable entity to determine a time horizon for a given DEI-related goal?
2. Have you informed the community of how much time they can expect the project to last from start to finish?
3. Did you develop check-in points, or milestones, between the starting point and reaching the desired outcome?
4. Did you meet the milestone at the given time, or is the project on schedule?
5. Does your process allow you to make incremental changes?

7

Conclusion

N ow that the model has been presented and described, you now have a framework for doing (or engaging) DEI-related work. The value of the model presented in this primer is that it forces individuals to write out a logical plan to assist with planning, carrying out, and evaluating DEI-related processes. To be sure, I will list the steps of the model here as a reminder.

1. What area of DEI do you want to advance?
2. What are your intended outcomes associated with the identified DEI area?
3. What are the metrics you will use to evaluate change?
4. What resources are needed to advance DEI toward the desired outcome?
5. Who is accountable for the DEI-related changes?
6. What is the time horizon for the DEI-related changes?

While the steps of the model have been listed and described in sequential order, it is also important to point out that DEI-related work, or at least some of its elements, is likely to not be a linear process. Rather, DEI programs are embedded in a system or systems that may require indirect efforts, with results that are not always clear. Or, maybe there are processes that require incremental adjustments and going to another part of the model before moving forward to other parts. For instance, say there is an ongoing DEI effort that has all of the steps, but a new person is hired who has a unique set of knowledge or skill that requires using a different metric. That "small" change may result in changes in other, or all, of the other steps in the model. In such cases, incremental changes should encourage evaluations of potential changes in the other steps of the model, and with collaborative approaches there can at least be genuine and honest conversation about how such changes can impact other processes (e.g., using the same example, maybe the new metric requires a longer wait between assessments, so this likely adjusts the time horizon).

Another point I would like to remind the reader and others doing DEI work in complex institutions of is that this model is not designed to give you the "right answer" to a problem in your institution as it relates to DEI-related processes. Rather, the intention of this model is to help leaders and constituents think through complex DEI-related changes and enact them in a way that reduces the amount of untended consequences that visions without a plan can result in. It would be notoriously difficult to specify a universal plan that works for all aspects of DEI across all institutions. However, what can work is developing processes for thinking about context-specific DEI-related goals and engaging community members in processes that increase the chances of realizing them and making the institution more diverse, equitable, and inclusive for all.

Appendix A

Logic Model Example

A Model for DEI Processes at Miami University

1. Identify and clarify the area of DEI you want to advance. Identify the current state of a given DEI area of the institution. This includes clearly conceptualizing the area of DEI being examined.
2. Articulate the intended changes (outcomes) for this area of the institution and the rationale for why the changes are needed (e.g., current state of affairs does not align with the strategic vision or mission of the university). Put differently, spell out where the institution is at (i.e., the "here") and where you want the institution to be (i.e., the "there"). This specifies the intended direction. Identifying any evidence to support advancing DEI in this would strengthen the argument being made.
3. Identify the metrics to be used to determine the extent of the intended changes. Focus groups, surveys, polls, internal versus external evaluators, how long of an evaluation period, and so on—all of these are critical to helping determine if the intended change is actually occurring.
4. Identify the expected resources, or costs, needed to enact the intended changes. Note possible unintended consequences as a result of attempting to enact intended changes.
5. Identify the person or entity in the institution that will be accountable for the desired DEI-related changes. Be sure there is a plan to regularly update the community on the status of the DEI-related work.

6. Articulate a clear time horizon for the intended change so that movement can be evaluated. Develop an evaluation schedule that includes benchmarks between the here and there.

If your ideas for DEI-related change cannot be mapped into this six-stage model, it would be prudent to figure out how to address the gaps before starting to advance changes. This model also allows for processes that not only point the DEI group in the direction of their hoped for or desired change but also prevents the group from being blinded by the unintended effects, which has historically derailed the advancement of DEI efforts. Finally, it is important to point out the assumptions in thinking guiding the intended changes. Again, the hope is that engaging in such processes help reduce leaders, or DEI groups, from being blinded to unintended outcomes.

Appendix B

Operational Processes for DEI-Related Work

Though the model is explained, some DEI-related entity may need more specific instructions for how to carry out the work. This appendix provides a guiding framework for the group.

Guiding Principles of the DEI Group

The first step for the group is to determine the guiding principles for the work they are doing. This is going to vary across institutions, but they should be tailored to the specific context in which the work is being done. To give an example, I have provided the five pillars outlined by the president of my university, which guided the work of the task force he commissioned and developed the recommendations that would be presented to the university leadership team. Upon submission of the recommendations to the president, an implementation group was convened to advance the recommendations. That group then took the pillars and collapsed them into broader areas. The point for sharing these steps is not to give you an absolute approach, but merely an example illustration using my experience. It would behoove you, and your institution, to do what works best in your given context. Also, be sure to save all documents so that as the work proceeds there is a way for new members on the various committees to have a way to get background knowledge about the work, know where it currently stands, and understand how to move forward.

Task Force Pillars:

1. Dialogue and allyship
2. Cultural consciousness
3. Advocacy and partnerships

4.   Structural and resource support
5.   Inclusion and accountability

Membership Across the Bucket Groups

Depending on how expansive the work is, it is likely to have subcommittees that will work on a set of recommendations or priorities or areas. Following is a simple table that can be used to help list members and the committees they are assigned to. There are spaces for members, and the Responsibility column is to assign particular areas (recommendations in my case) that each group was to work on. It may be helpful to also communicate this to the community so they can reach out to given individuals/ groups if they have inquiries.

	Members	Members	Responsibility
Dialogue and allyship (Team leader)			
Cultural consciousness (Team leader)			
Advocacy and partnerships (Team leader)			
Structural and resource supports (Team leader)			
Inclusion and accountability (Team leader)			

Group Operational Procedures

For any committee, there will need to be rules for operations. Using the same example as the previous section, I have provided the same operational rules I provided to committee members. This list is not exhaustive or absolute; feel free to edit it as necessary to fit what works best in your institutional context.

1. **Intragroup dynamics (subgroups):** Develop rules for the group and be consistent. Examples include selecting if your group will have a leader who coordinates all of the work or if everyone will take a leading role. Have a designed person(s) to make updates to the document that lists all of the topics/goals/recommendations. Being consistent includes making sure there are not too many voices coming outside of the group, such as having too many people contacting a given accountable party about a given topic/goal/recommendation. That can be confusing and overwhelming. This will be helpful as the work moves forward and transitions to the next phase. Each meeting there will be time in our bucket groups to discuss updates on work toward goals. The group should have prepared some notes to update the full committee on given recommendations or goals. Note that you do not have to provide an update on each task or goal, each week, just an update on those that have seen some movement. Be sure to update the notes in the shared document.

2. **Intergroup dynamics (full implementation group):** Each week there will be an allotment of time for the full implementation team to meet and discuss updates across the group areas and to report to the larger group challenges and other updates. Committee chairs will also provide any updates they have received from given entities around campus (e.g., communicating any notes from the president's executive cabinet). This is also a time to share information with other groups you are knowledgeable about that are outside the purview of the working group you are assigned. The goal is for people to have a working knowledge of what is going on across all of the groups, with a deeper knowledge about things in their assigned bucket groups.

3. **Framework when reaching out to campus partners:** Once you have developed rules for reaching out, be sure to reach out to the accountable parties about a given recommendation. Use the steps in the model as a guide for structuring the conversation you have

with accountable parties when you reach out to them. This is a guide for moving the work forward. Questions that arise during communication can be discussed at the full group meeting. In short, there will be barriers (e.g., resources, time) for moving some recommendations forward, and using this model will help identify them so that committee chairs can speak with upper administration about those barriers.

    i.   *Identify the area of DEI being addressed.*

    ii.   *Articulate intended outcomes.*

    iii. *Determine metrics of change.*

    iv. *Note resources needed to achieve expected outcomes.*

    v.   *Establish a clear time horizon for reaching the intended outcome.*

    vi. *Assign an entity or individual(s) accountable for the suggested change process*

4. **Goal when reaching out to campus partners:** Some may have questions about what they should be doing when reaching out to campus partners. Essentially, we want to advance the recommendation or understand why it would not be feasible to reach the intended outcome listed in the recommendation. Either way, we must report back to the community with an update. In reaching out, there are (at least) two possible scenarios that arise:

    a.   Simply discuss the ideas with the accountable entity and determine what work is being done that is related to the recommendations or goals (again, see the framework to determine questions to discuss). For this scenario, the work is being progressed and we keep in touch to get updates or see if we need to discuss resources to meet the outcome or connect the accountable office to another office on campus and help them think through how to move the work forward.

    b.   The implementation group has key information or knowledge to help the accountable party move the work forward. For instance, have there been conversations about the goals that would be helpful to the accountable entity? If so, share that.

5. **Community updates:** Always have a plan to update the community. The task force I co-led suggested having quarterly updates by the team leaders; however, establish a schedule that works best for your institutional contexts. Suggested platforms include

social media, websites, and email lists. It is also helpful to have the progression of the work housed on a website for tracking updates.

6. **Media inquiries:** You may receive media inquiries about the work. Work with your communications and marketing teams about how to navigate those. Keep in mind that not all people share your enthusiasm for the work and may have vastly different agendas.

7. **Psychological safe space:** Please keep discussions in the committee meetings confidential. Of course, some information will be given to campus partners as that is part of the information exchange needed to move this work forward. However, some things are not public and should remain in the group. If there are questions, please raise them in the full group meeting so we can develop a plan. All members must feel safe raising valid concerns, even disagreements, about the work, and that information cannot be leaked. It can derail the work when people shut down and are not open and honest about the promise and/or constraints to advancing the work.

8. **Transition:** Have a clear plan for transitioning the work to future groups or to an endpoint. This will also help with setting goals and benchmarks along the way. Clearly communicate that to the team so that people are aware of their time commitment and what to expect moving forward.

9. **Gratitude:** As leaders, always always, always show gratitude for the work people do in this realm. It is difficult work and taxing in many ways.

References

Campbell, D. P. (1990). *If you don't know where you're going, you'll probably end up somewhere else.* Thomas More Association. https://www.amazon.com/Where-Youre-Going-Probably-Somewhere/dp/0883473275

Dobbin, F., & Kalev, A. (2016). Why diversity programs fail. *Harvard Business Review, 94*(7), 52–6014. https://stratserv.co/wp-content/uploads/2020/08/Why-Diversity-Programs-Fail.pdf

European Commission (2003). *The costs and benefits of diversity: A study on methods and indicators to measure the cost-effectiveness of diversity policies in enterprises.*

Ford, D. H., & Lerner, R. M. (1992). *Developmental systems theory: An integrative approach.* SAGE.

Gopalan, M., & Brady, S. T. (2020). College students' sense of belonging: A national perspective. *Educational Researcher, 49*(2), 134–137.

Jaccard, J., & Jacoby, J. (2019). *Theory construction and model-building skills: A practical guide for social scientists.* Guilford.

James, A. G. (2020). *Black families: A systems approach.* Cognella.

Mac Donald, H. (2018). *The diversity delusion: How race and gender pandering corrupt the university and undermine our culture.* St. Martin's Press.

Miami University (2018). Office of Institutional Research: Fact sheet 2018. https://www.miamioh.edu/oir/_files/documents/fbook/fsheet/fs2018.pdf

O'Reilly, J., Robinson, S. L., Berdahl, J. L., & Banki, S. (2015). Is negative attention better than no attention? The comparative effects of ostracism and harassment at work. *Organization Science, 26*(3), 774–793.

Osborne, J. W., & Waters, E. (2002). Four assumptions of multiple regression that researchers should always test. *Practical Assessment, Research & Evaluation, 8*(2). https://scholarworks.umass.edu/pare/vol8/iss1/2/

Reiners, B. (2020, July 31). *Types of diversity in the workplace you need to know: A guide to 34 unique diversity characteristics.* Built In. https://builtin.com/diversity-inclusion/types-of-diversity-in-the-workplace

Rossi, P. H., Lipsey, M. W., & Henry, G. T. (2018). *Evaluation: A systematic approach.* SAGE.

Sowell, T. (2002). *A conflict of visions: Ideological origins of political struggles*. Basic Books.

Sowell, T. (2008). *Applied economics: Thinking beyond stage one*. Basic Books.

Sowell, T. (2019). *Discrimination and disparities*. Basic Books.

Tschirhart, M., & Bielefeld, W. (2012). *Managing nonprofit organizations*. Wiley.

U.S. Department of Labor. (n.d). *Disaggregating minority groups for AAP placement goals*. Office of Federal Contract Compliance Programs. https://www.dol.gov/agencies/ofccp/faqs/placement-goals

Wheelan, C. (2013). *Naked statistics: Stripping the dread from the data*. Norton.

Index

G

goal, 40
governing boards, 6–7
gratitude, 41
group operational procedures, 39–41
guiding principles of DEI group, 37–38

I

inclusion, 9–10, 27–28. *See also* diversity, equity, and inclusion (DEI)
Inclusion and Diversity Committee, 3
incremental approaches, 22
institution, 25–26
intergroup dynamics, 39
intragroup dynamics, 39
Iraq, 2

K

Kalev, Anaokulu, 20

L

logic model example, 35–36

M

media inquiries, 41
membership, 38–39
metrics of change, 21–22
Miami University, 2, 3, 6, 8, 12, 17, 35–36
Missouri Department of Social Services, 2

N

nonprofit agencies, 1
nontenure track (NTT), 4–5. *See also* tenure-track (TT)

O

Operation Iraqi Freedom campaign, 2
opportunities, 3
outcomes, 19–20

support or rationale for, 19–20
unintended, 20
vs. process, 10

P

PDF files, 17
Presidential Task Force, 3
process *vs.* outcome, 10
psychological safe space, 41

R

Reiners, Braun, 16
resource costs, 25–26
resources for changes, 24–26

S

social organizations, 1
Sowell, Thomas, 13
staff, 5
students, 4, 10

T

tenure-track (TT), 4–5
time horizon, 30–32
    be realistic, 31–32
    be reasonable, 31–32
    determining, 30–31
    focus on process, 32
transition, 41

U

unintended outcomes, 20
University of Missouri, 3
university structure, 3–7
    administrators, 5–6
    alumni, 6
    faculty, 4–5
    governing boards, 6–7
    staff, 5
    students, 4